THE COMPLETE HEALTHY SMOOTHIE RECIPE BOOK

Table of Contents

Introduction

Thank you for purchasing *The Complete Healthy Smoothie Recipe Book.*

If you are tired of carrying around those excess pounds and are seeking ways to feel your best in a colorful, easy way, then smoothies are a perfect go-to!

This book is loaded with over 100 delicious, easy-to-make smoothie recipes that will help you much more than just melting off that weight you wish to lose! From boosting your energy to making your skin more radiant, these smoothie recipes are a fool-proof way to get you back on track with your overall health.

While there are tons of smoothie books on the market today, there are none quite like this one! Thank you again for choosing this book.   Every effort was made to ensure it is full of as much useful information as possible, please enjoy!

Healthy Heart

1. Carrot Papaya Protein Smoothie

Ingredients:

- 4 ice cubes
- ½ C. berries of choice
- ¼ C. carrot juice
- 1 scoop of whey protein, your choice of flavor
- ½ papaya

Here's how to do it:

1. Mix everything in a blender.
2. Puree ingredients until smooth in texture or you reach your desired consistency.

2. Blueberry Avocado Protein Smoothie

Ingredients:

- 4 ice cubes
- ½ an avocado
- 1 C. frozen blueberries
- 1 scoop whey protein, your choice of flavor
- 1 C. coconut water

Here's how to do it:

1. Mix everything in a blender.
2. Puree ingredients until smooth in texture or you reach your desired consistency.

3. Chia Seed Acai Berry Protein Smoothie

Ingredients:

- 1 scoop whey protein, your choice of flavor
- 2 tbsp. chia seeds
- 3 ounces frozen acai berries
- 2 C. unsweetened almond milk

Here's how to do it:

1. Mix everything in a blender.
2. Puree ingredients until smooth in texture or you reach your desired consistency.

4. Banana Oat Protein Smoothie

Ingredients:

- 4 ice cubes
- 1 scoop whey protein, your choice of flavor
- 1 tsp. honey
- ¼ tsp. cinnamon
- 1 C. unsweetened almond milk
- 4 tbsp. rolled oats
- 2 bananas

Here's how to do it:

1. Mix everything in a blender.
2. Puree ingredients until smooth in texture or you reach your desired consistency.

5. Chocolate Peanut Butter Protein Smoothie

Ingredients:

- 1 C. low-fat yogurt
- 1 scoop whey protein, your choice of flavor
- 1 frozen banana
- 2 tbsp. 100% chocolate syrup
- 2 tbsp. peanut butter
- ½ C. low-fat milk

Here's how to do it:

1. Mix everything in a blender.
2. Puree ingredients until smooth in texture or you reach your desired consistency.

6. Green Flax Smoothie

Ingredients:

- ½ C. frozen pineapple chunks
- 2 C. spinach
- 1 banana
- 2 peeled clementines
- 2 tbsp. flax seeds
- ½ C. water

Here's how to do it:

1. Mix everything in a blender.
2. Puree ingredients until smooth in texture or you reach your desired consistency.

7. The Healthy Start Smoothie

Ingredients:

- 1 C. ice cubes
- ¾ C. frozen mango chunks
- 1 C. fresh pineapple chunks
- 1 ½ C. kale
- 1 tbsp. agave nectar
- 1 tbsp. chia seeds
- ½ C. low-fat cottage cheese
- 6 ounces water

Here's how to do it:

1. Mix everything in a blender.
2. Puree ingredients until smooth in texture or you reach your desired consistency.

8. Fudgesicle Frosty Smoothie

Ingredients:

- 3 C. ice cubes
- ½ of a peeled/pitted avocado
- 4 pitted Medjool dates
- 1/3 C. cocoa powder
- ¼ C. agave nectar
- 2/3 C. coconut milk

Here's how to do it:

1. Mix everything in a blender.
2. Puree ingredients until smooth in texture or you reach your desired consistency.

9. Orange Julicious Smoothie

Ingredients:

- 1 tsp. vanilla extract
- 2 tbsp. honey
- 6 ounces frozen orange juice concentrate
- 1 ½ C. ice cubes
- 1 C. yellow squash
- 2 peeled oranges
- 1 C. low-fat milk

Here's how to do it:

1. Mix everything in a blender.
2. Puree ingredients until smooth in texture or you reach your desired consistency.

10. Green Monster Smoothie

Ingredients:

- 1 C. ice cubes
- 1 C. frozen mango
- 1 C. spinach
- 1 C. kale
- ½ banana
- 1 cored/quartered apple of choice
- 12 ounces orange juice

Here's how to do it:

1. Mix everything in a blender.
2. Puree ingredients until smooth in texture or you reach your desired consistency.

11. Red Rose Lemonade Smoothie

Ingredients:

- 1 C. ice
- 1 C. water
- 1 tsp. rose hips powder
- ½ an inch of ginger
- ½ juiced lemon
- 1 chopped apple of choice
- 4 ounces chopped beets

Here's how to do it:

1. Mix everything in a blender.
2. Puree ingredients until smooth in texture or you reach your desired consistency.

12. Fine-Apple Smoothie

Ingredients:

- 1 C. ice
- 1 C. water
- 3 tbsp. cashews
- 1 tbsp. yacon root
- 4 ounces cantaloupe
- 4 ounces pineapple
- 4 ounces grapes

Here's how to do it:

1. Mix everything in a blender.
2. Puree ingredients until smooth in texture or you reach your desired consistency.

13. "The Kiwi to My Heart" Smoothie

Ingredients:

- 1 C. ice
- 1 C. water
- 1 tbsp. hemp seeds
- 1 juiced lime
- 1 chopped cucumber
- 1 peeled kiwi
- 1 chopped pear
- 1 ½ ounces baby spinach

Here's how to do it:

1. Mix everything in a blender.
2. Puree ingredients until smooth in texture or you reach your desired consistency.

14. Spiced Orange Cider Smoothie

Ingredients:

- 1 C. ice
- 1 C. water
- ¼ tsp. ground cloves
- 1 tbsp. pea protein
- ½ juiced lemon
- 1 tbsp. apple cider vinegar
- ½ pitted avocado
- 2 peeled clementines
- 1 ½ ounces collard greens

Here's how to do it:

1. Mix everything in a blender.
2. Puree ingredients until smooth in texture or you reach your desired consistency.

15. Chocolate Covered Coconut Smoothie

Ingredients:

- 1 C. ice
- 1 C. coconut water
- 2 dates
- 1 ½ tbsp. cacao powder
- ½ pitted avocado
- 2 peeled bananas
- 1 ½ ounces swiss chard

Here's how to do it:

1. Mix everything in a blender.
2. Puree ingredients until smooth in texture or you reach your desired consistency.

Detoxification

1. Morning Magic Smoothie

Ingredients:

- Ice
- 1 tbsp. flax meal
- 1 scoop protein powder, flavor of choice
- 1/3 C. plain yogurt
- 1 frozen banana
- 1 C. cold coffee

Here's how to do it:

1. Mix everything in a blender.
2. Puree ingredients until smooth in texture or you reach your desired consistency.

2. Healthy Detox Smoothie

Ingredients:

- ½ C. coconut water
- ¼ cucumber
- ¼ C. blueberries
- 1 tbsp. fresh ginger
- 2-3 tbsp. lemon juice
- 1 C. spinach
- ½ frozen banana

Here's how to do it:

1. Mix everything in a blender.
2. Puree ingredients until smooth in texture or you reach your desired consistency.

3. Anti-Bloat Smoothie

Ingredients:

- Ice
- 1 tsp. apple cider vinegar
- 1-2 tbsp. fresh ginger
- ½ cucumber
- 1 frozen banana
- ½ C. coconut water

Here's how to do it:

1. Mix everything in a blender.
2. Puree ingredients until smooth in texture or you reach your desired consistency.

4. Green Detox Smoothie

Ingredients:

- 1 C. cold water
- 1 C. unsweetened almond milk
- ½ - 1 tsp. spirulina powder
- 2 tbsp. chia seeds
- 1 C. frozen pineapple
- 1 frozen ripe banana
- 1 peeled lemon
- 2 chopped celery stalks
- ½ chopped cucumber
- 1 ½ C. kale

Here's how to do it:

1. Mix everything in a blender.
2. Puree ingredients until smooth in texture or you reach your desired consistency.

5. Sunrise Detox Smoothie

Ingredients:

- 1 C. coconut water
- ½ C. frozen raspberries
- ½ C. pineapple
- ½ C. frozen mango
- 1 frozen banana
- Juice of 1 lemon

Here's how to do it:

1. Blend raspberries and set to the side.
2. Blend remaining ingredients until smooth.
3. Pour raspberry mixture into serving glass first, followed by mango mixture.

5-Ingredient Detox Smoothie

Ingredients:

- 1 C. fruit juice of choice (orange, pomegranate, etc.)
- 1 tbsp. flax seed meal
- ½ C. frozen banana
- 1 C. kale or spinach
- 1 C. frozen berries of choice

Here's how to do it:

1. Mix everything in a blender.
2. Puree ingredients until smooth in texture or you reach your desired consistency.

6. Golden Detox Smoothie

Ingredients:

- Ice cubes
- ½ C. water
- ½ C. orange juice, freshly squeezed
- ½ C. fresh pineapple
- 1 peeled/diced carrot
- 2 tbsp. honey Greek yogurt
- 1 banana

Here's how to do it:

1. Mix everything in a blender.
2. Puree ingredients until smooth in texture or you reach your desired consistency.

7. Kale Recharge Smoothie

Ingredients:

- 4 ice cubes
- 1 C. water
- 1 tsp. lime juice
- 1 tbsp. parsley
- 1 tsp. grated ginger
- ½ C. chopped carrots
- ¾ C. kale
- ¾ C. spinach
- 1 frozen ripe banana

Here's how to do it:

1. Mix everything in a blender.
2. Puree ingredients until smooth in texture or you reach your desired consistency.

8. Toxic Blast Cleansing Smoothie

Ingredients:

- ½ C. water
- 2-3 ice cubes
- ½ C. strawberries, cored
- 1 banana
- 1 C. blueberries
- 1 handful spinach

Here's how to do it:

1. Mix everything in a blender.
2. Puree ingredients until smooth in texture or you reach your desired consistency.

9. Apple and Kale Green Detox Smoothie

Ingredients:

- 1 tsp. honey
- 1 tbsp. ground flax seed
- ½ green or red apple, cored/chopped
- 1 chopped celery stalk
- 1 ½ C. chopped kale
- ¾ C. ice
- 2/3 C. unsweetened almond milk

Here's how to do it:

1. Mix everything in a blender.
2. Puree ingredients until smooth in texture or you reach your desired consistency.

10. Sweet Spirit Smoothie

Ingredients:

- 1 scoop vanilla protein powder
- 1 tsp. spirulina
- ½ C. almond milk
- ¼ avocado
- ½ C. blueberries
- ½ banana

Here's how to do it:

1. Mix everything in a blender.
2. Puree ingredients until smooth in texture or you reach your desired consistency.

11. Alkalinity Bliss Smoothie

Ingredients:

- 1 scoop protein powder, your choice of flavor
- 1 tsp. chia seeds
- 1 C. almond milk
- ¼ C. coconut water
- 1 packed cup of spinach
- ¼ avocado
- ½ pear

Here's how to do it:

1. Mix everything in a blender.
2. Puree ingredients until smooth in texture or you reach your desired consistency.

12. Strawberry Fields Smoothie

Ingredients:

- 1 ½ C. spinach
- 1 banana
- 1 peeled orange
- 1 tbsp. lemon zest
- 2 C. strawberries
- 3 C. cashew milk

Here's how to do it:

1. Mix everything in a blender.
2. Puree ingredients until smooth in texture or you reach your desired consistency.

13. Sicilian Smoothie

Ingredients:

- 1 seeded red jalapeno pepper
- 1 C. spinach
- 1 C. watercress
- 4 celery stalks
- 4 garlic cloves
- 2 red bell peppers
- 3 tomatoes
- 6 carrots

Here's how to do it:

1. Mix everything in a blender.
2. Puree ingredients until smooth in texture or you reach your desired consistency.

14. Lemon Blueberry Smoothie

Ingredients:

- 1 lemon
- ¼ C. blueberries
- 1 C. alkaline water

Here's how to do it:

1. Mix everything in a blender.
2. Puree ingredients until smooth in texture or you reach your desired consistency.

Weight Loss

1. Blueberry Smoothie

Ingredients:

- 1 tbsp. flax seed oil
- 1 banana
- 1 C. blueberries

Here's how to do it:

1. Mix everything in a blender.
2. Puree ingredients until smooth in texture or you reach your desired consistency.

2. Chocolate Raspberry Smoothie

Ingredients:

- ½ C. unsweetened almond milk
- ¼ C. chocolate chips
- 1 C. raspberries

Here's how to do it:

1. Mix everything in a blender.
2. Puree ingredients until smooth in texture or you reach your desired consistency.

3. Silky Mango Smoothie

Ingredients:

- 2 C. mango
- ½ C. avocado
- 1 C. fresh orange juice
- ¼ C. lime juice

Here's how to do it:

1. Mix everything in a blender.
2. Puree ingredients until smooth in texture or you reach your desired consistency.

4. Green Almond Smoothie

Ingredients:

- ½ C. unsweetened almond milk
- ¼ C. natural almond butter
- 1 banana
- 1 ½ C. kale

Here's how to do it:

1. Mix everything in a blender.
2. Puree ingredients until smooth in texture or you reach your desired consistency.

5. Lemon Orange Citrus Smoothie

Ingredients:

- ½ C. skim milk
- ¼ C. lemon yogurt
- 1 peeled orange
- 2 tbsp. flax seed oil
- 3-4 ice cubes

Here's how to do it:

1. Mix everything in a blender.
2. Puree ingredients until smooth in texture or you reach your desired consistency.

6. Apple Blaster Smoothie

Ingredients:

- ½ C. water
- 2 celery stalks
- 1-inch piece ginger, grated
- 3 carrots
- 2 apples of choice

Here's how to do it:

1. Mix everything in a blender.
2. Puree ingredients until smooth in texture or you reach your desired consistency.

7. All-Rounder Smoothie

Ingredients:

- 1 thumb of grated ginger
- Handful of spinach
- 1 C. water
- 1 lemon

Here's how to do it:

1. Mix everything in a blender.
2. Puree ingredients until smooth in texture or you reach your desired consistency.

8. Fat Burning Green Smoothie

Ingredients:

- 1 tbsp. chia seeds
- ½ tsp. ginger
- 1 C. frozen pineapple chunks
- 1 C. unsweetened almond milk
- 1 banana
- 2 handfuls baby spinach

Here's how to do it:

1. Mix everything in a blender.
2. Puree ingredients until smooth in texture or you reach your desired consistency.

9. Mango Passion Fruit Smoothie

Ingredients:

- 1 ½ C. orange juice
- 1 mango
- 1 banana
- 3 passion fruits

Here's how to do it:

1. Mix everything in a blender.
2. Puree ingredients until smooth in texture or you reach your desired consistency.

10. Fruity Green Smoothie

Ingredients:

- 1 tsp. lemon juice
- 1 tsp. grated ginger
- 1 ½ C. water
- 1 chopped pear
- 2 C. spinach

Here's how to do it:

1. Mix everything in a blender.
2. Puree ingredients until smooth in texture or you reach your desired consistency.

11. Kale Chia Seed Smoothie

Ingredients:

- 1 tsp. lemon juice
- 1 C. plain yogurt
- 1 tbsp. chia seeds
- 1 banana
- 2 kale leaves

Here's how to do it:

1. Mix everything in a blender.
2. Puree ingredients until smooth in texture or you reach your desired consistency.

12. Zesty Fat Burner Smoothie

Ingredients:

- 1 tbsp. flax seeds
- 1 C. water
- 1 lemon
- 3 slices of pineapple

Here's how to do it:

1. Mix everything in a blender.
2. Puree ingredients until smooth in texture or you reach your desired consistency.

13. Matcha Pear Green Protein Smoothie

Ingredients:

- ½ tsp. matcha tea powder
- 1 pear
- 1 C. spinach
- 1 C. unsweetened almond milk
- 2 scoops vanilla protein powder

Here's how to do it:

1. Mix everything in a blender.
2. Puree ingredients until smooth in texture or you reach your desired consistency.

14. Watermelon Smoothie

Ingredients:

- 12 ice cubes
- 1 C. lemon sherbet
- 6 C. seedless watermelon

Here's how to do it:

1. Mix everything in a blender.
2. Puree ingredients until smooth in texture or you reach your desired consistency.

15. Spinach Avocado Smoothie

Ingredients:

- 1 C. water
- 1 tbsp. peanut butter
- 1 banana
- 1 C. spinach
- 1 avocado

Here's how to do it:

1. Mix everything in a blender.
2. Puree ingredients until smooth in texture or you reach your desired consistency.

Radiant Skin

1. Powerhouse Pumpkin Smoothie

Ingredients:

- ½ tsp. pumpkin pie spice
- 2 tbsp. ground flaxseed
- ¼ avocado
- ½ C. water
- 7 ounces 2% Greek yogurt
- ½ C. canned pure pumpkin

Here's how to do it:

1. Mix everything in a blender.
2. Puree ingredients until smooth in texture or you reach your desired consistency.

2. Mango Surprise Smoothie

Ingredients:

- 6 ice cubes
- 1 tbsp. sugar
- 1 tbsp. lime juice
- ¼ C. fat-free vanilla yogurt
- ¼ C. mashed avocado
- ¼ C. mango cubes
- ½ C. mango juice

Here's how to do it:

1. Mix everything in a blender.
2. Puree ingredients until smooth in texture or you reach your desired consistency.

3. Super Green Smoothie

Ingredients:

- ¼ C. chopped mint
- ¼ C. chopped parsley
- 1 C. chilled orange juice
- 2 chopped celery ribs
- 1 ¼ C. frozen cubed mango
- 1 ¼ C. chopped kale

Here's how to do it:

1. Mix everything in a blender.
2. Puree ingredients until smooth in texture or you reach your desired consistency.

4. Gingered Cantaloupe Smoothie

Ingredients:

- ½ tsp. grated ginger
- 3 tbsp. sugar
- 6 ounces low-fat plain yogurt
- 2 C. cubed cantaloupe
- 20 ice cubes

Here's how to do it:

1. Mix everything in a blender.
2. Puree ingredients until smooth in texture or you reach your desired consistency.

5. Healthy High C Smoothie

Ingredients:

- ¼ C. ice cubes
- 1 chopped celery rib
- ½ C. cilantro sprigs
- ½ C. orange or tangerine juice
- 2 peeled/chopped kiwis
- 1 C. chopped kale

Here's how to do it:

1. Mix everything in a blender.
2. Puree ingredients until smooth in texture or you reach your desired consistency.

6. Carrot Cake Smoothie

Ingredients:

- Ice cubes
- 2g glucomannan
- ¼ tsp. cinnamon
- 1 tsp. flaxseed oil
- 1 tbsp. softened cream cheese
- 2 tbsp. toasted wheat germ
- 1 scoop vanilla protein powder
- ½ C. unsweetened carrot juice

Here's how to do it:

1. Mix everything in a blender.
2. Puree ingredients until smooth in texture or you reach your desired consistency.

7. Winter Greens Smoothie

Ingredients:

- 1 cored/chopped apple
- 1 frozen/peeled/sliced banana
- 4 sliced/frozen broccoli florets
- 1 C. chopped kale
- 1 C. spinach
- ½ C. orange juice
- ¼ C. carrot juice

Here's how to do it:

1. Mix everything in a blender.
2. Puree ingredients until smooth in texture or you reach your desired consistency.

8. Apricot Smoothie

Ingredients:

- 1/8 tsp. almond extract
- 2/3 C. non-fat vanilla frozen yogurt
- 1 C. skim milk
- 12 pitted apricot halves

Here's how to do it:

1. Mix everything in a blender.
2. Puree ingredients until smooth in texture or you reach your desired consistency.

9. Veggie and Fruit Smoothie

Ingredients:

- 6 baby carrots
- ½ sliced banana
- 1 C. spinach
- 1 C. frozen berries
- ½ C. low-fat vanilla yogurt
- ½ C. orange juice

Here's how to do it:

1. Mix everything in a blender.
2. Puree ingredients until smooth in texture or you reach your desired consistency.

10. Green Goddess Smoothie

Ingredients:

- ¼ C. mint leaves
- ½ C. orange juice
- ½ C. frozen vanilla yogurt
- 1 peeled/chopped kiwi
- ½ peeled avocado
- 1 C. cucumber chunks
- 1 C. baby spinach

Here's how to do it:

1. Mix everything in a blender.
2. Puree ingredients until smooth in texture or you reach your desired consistency.

11. Cinnamon Apple Crumble Smoothie

Ingredients:

- 1 C. ice
- 1 C. water
- ¼ C. walnuts
- 1 tbsp. quinoa flakes
- 1 tsp. cinnamon
- 2 chopped apples
- 1 ½ ounces swiss chard

Here's how to do it:

1. Mix everything in a blender.
2. Puree ingredients until smooth in texture or you reach your desired consistency.

12. Celery Apple Refresher Smoothie

Ingredients:

- 1 C. ice
- 1 C. water
- ½ tsp. moringa
- 2 tbsp. raw hazelnuts
- 3 sprigs of mint
- 1 chopped apple
- 2 celery ribs
- 1 ½ ounce collard greens

Here's how to do it:

1. Mix everything in a blender.
2. Puree ingredients until smooth in texture or you reach your desired consistency.

13. Summer Strawberry Sunset Smoothie

Ingredients:

- 1 C. ice
- 1 C. vanilla almond milk
- 1 tbsp. coconut flakes
- 1 peeled blood orange
- 1 chopped pear
- 1 C. strawberries

Here's how to do it:

1. Mix everything in a blender.
2. Puree ingredients until smooth in texture or you reach your desired consistency.

14. Ginger Plum Flower Smoothie

Ingredients:

- 1 C. ice
- 1 C. water
- 1 tbsp. chia seeds
- ½ juiced lemon
- ½ an inch of peeled ginger
- 2 pitted plums
- 1 peeled orange
- 4 ounces chopped beets

Here's how to do it:

1. Mix everything in a blender.
2. Puree ingredients until smooth in texture or you reach your desired consistency.

15. Yellow Turmeric Ginger Smoothie

Ingredients:

- 1 C. ice
- 1 C. water
- 1 tbsp. hemp seed
- ½ an inch peeled ginger
- ½ tsp. turmeric
- 1-ounce of kumquats
- 1 peeled orange
- 1 chopped yellow squash

Here's how to do it:

1. Mix everything in a blender.
2. Puree ingredients until smooth in texture or you reach your desired consistency.

Energy Boost

1. Mango, Mandarin, Cayenne Smoothie

Ingredients:

- 1 tsp. vanilla
- 1/8 tsp. cayenne powder
- 1 tbsp. honey
- 1 C. mango chunks
- 1 peeled/seeded mandarin orange
- 1 C. unsweetened almond milk

Here's how to do it:

1. Mix everything in a blender.
2. Puree ingredients until smooth in texture or you reach your desired consistency.

2. Key Lime Pie Smoothie

Ingredients:

- 2 tbsp. honey
- 1 tsp. vanilla
- 2 bananas
- 1 avocado
- ½ C. lime juice
- 1 ½ C. apple juice

Here's how to do it:

1. Mix everything in a blender.
2. Puree ingredients until smooth in texture or you reach your desired consistency.

3. Banana, Mint, Coconut Water Smoothie

Ingredients:

- 1 tsp. vanilla
- 1 tbsp. hemp seeds
- 2 C. coconut water
- 1 handful mint leaves
- 5 frozen bananas

Here's how to do it:

1. Mix everything in a blender.
2. Puree ingredients until smooth in texture or you reach your desired consistency.

4. Raspberry, Cacao, Maca Smoothie

Ingredients:

- ½ tsp. cinnamon
- 1 tsp. lucuma powder
- 1 tsp. vanilla
- 1 tsp. maca powder
- ¼ C. cashews
- 1 tbsp. raw cacao nibs
- 1 C. baby spinach
- ½ C. frozen raspberries

Here's how to do it:

1. Mix everything in a blender.
2. Puree ingredients until smooth in texture or you reach your desired consistency.

5. Ginger, Pear, Lemongrass Smoothie

Ingredients:

- 2 C. coconut milk
- 1 tsp. raw honey
- ¼ inch ginger root
- 1-2 stalks lemongrass
- 1 frozen banana
- 1 cored pear

Here's how to do it:

1. Mix everything in a blender.
2. Puree ingredients until smooth in texture or you reach your desired consistency.

6. Banana, Turmeric, Chai Smoothie

Ingredients:

- ¼ inch turmeric root
- ¼ inch ginger root
- 1 tsp. vanilla
- 1 tsp. lucuma powder
- 1-2 tsp. raw honey
- ¼ C. rolled oats
- 2 C. chilled chai tea
- 2 frozen bananas

Here's how to do it:

1. Mix everything in a blender.
2. Puree ingredients until smooth in texture or you reach your desired consistency.

7. Forest Berry and Brazil Nut Smoothie

Ingredients:

- 2 C. apple juice
- 1 tsp. guarana powder
- ¼ C. Brazil nuts
- 1 C. baby spinach
- 1 frozen banana
- 2 C. frozen mixed berries
- Raw honey, to taste

Here's how to do it:

1. Mix everything in a blender.
2. Puree ingredients until smooth in texture or you reach your desired consistency.
3. Adjust sweetness of smoothie with raw honey.

8. Chocolate, Chia, Banana Smoothie

Ingredients:

- 1 tsp. lucuma powder
- 1 tsp. vanilla
- 2 C. walnut milk
- 1 tbsp. raw cacao nibs
- 2 tbsp. soaked chia seeds
- 1 C. baby spinach
- 2 frozen bananas

Here's how to do it:

1. Mix everything in a blender.
2. Puree ingredients until smooth in texture or you reach your desired consistency.

9. Banana Matcha Energizing Smoothie

Ingredients:

- 1-2 tsp. honey
- 1-2 tsp. matcha powder
- 2 C. almond milk
- 1 C. romaine lettuce
- 2 frozen bananas

Here's how to do it:

1. Mix everything in a blender.
2. Puree ingredients until smooth in texture or you reach your desired consistency.

10. Kale and Lavender Energizing Smoothie

Ingredients:

- 1 tsp. vanilla
- 1 tsp. lucuma powder
- ¼ C. raw cashews
- ½ C. rolled oats
- 1 C. apple juice
- 1 C. kale
- 1 C. mulberries
- 1 frozen banana

Here's how to do it:

1. Mix everything in a blender.
2. Puree ingredients until smooth in texture or you reach your desired consistency.

11. Peach Vanilla Yogurt Smoothie

Ingredients:

- ½ C. non-fat vanilla frozen yogurt
- 1 peach
- 1 C. soy milk

Here's how to do it:

1. Mix everything in a blender.
2. Puree ingredients until smooth in texture or you reach your desired consistency.

12. Berry Vanilla Banana Smoothie

Ingredients:

- ¼ tsp. vanilla
- ½ frozen banana
- ¼ C. frozen red grapes
- ¼ C. frozen blackberries
- ¼ C. frozen blueberries
- 1/3 C. 1%-fat cottage cheese
- 1 C. non-fat milk

Here's how to do it:

1. Mix everything in a blender.
2. Puree ingredients until smooth in texture or you reach your desired consistency.

13. Green Grape Smoothie

Ingredients:

- 2 C. ice
- ½ C. water
- 1 tsp. chia seeds
- 1 banana
- 1 peeled orange
- 1 cored pear
- 1 C. green grapes
- 1 C. chopped kale
- 1 C. spinach

Here's how to do it:

1. Mix everything in a blender.
2. Puree ingredients until smooth in texture or you reach your desired consistency.

14. Peach and Orange Smoothie

Ingredients:

- 1 C. fat-free milk
- 2 tbsp. flaxseed
- ½ C. orange juice
- 2 C. sliced peaches
- 2 C. light ice cream

Here's how to do it:

1. Mix everything in a blender.
2. Puree ingredients until smooth in texture or you reach your desired consistency.

15. Mango Strawberry Smoothie

Ingredients:

- 1 tsp. chia seeds
- ¼ C. green tea
- 1 tbsp. Greek yogurt
- ¼ C. red bell pepper
- ¼ C. chopped carrot
- ¼ C. kale
- ¼ C. frozen peach slices
- ¼ C. red grapes
- ½ C. frozen mango
- 1 C. strawberries

Here's how to do it:

1. Mix everything in a blender.
2. Puree ingredients until smooth in texture or you reach your desired consistency.

Anti-Aging

1. Blueberry Breeze Smoothie

Ingredients:

- 1 handful mint
- 1 tsp. chia seeds
- 1 tbsp. lemon juice
- 1 C. coconut water
- 1 C. strawberries
- 1 C. frozen blueberries

Here's how to do it:

1. Mix everything in a blender.
2. Puree ingredients until smooth in texture or you reach your desired consistency.

2. Tropical Chia Smoothie

Ingredients:

- 1 C. coconut water
- 1 tbsp. chia seeds
- 1 C. pineapple
- ½ C. mango

Here's how to do it:

1. Mix everything in a blender.
2. Puree ingredients until smooth in texture or you reach your desired consistency.

3. Cacao Banana Dream Smoothie

Ingredients:

- 1 C. unsweetened almond milk
- 1 tbsp. cacao powder
- 6 strawberries
- 1 banana

Here's how to do it:

1. Mix everything in a blender.
2. Puree ingredients until smooth in texture or you reach your desired consistency.

4. Berry Power Smoothie

Ingredients:

- Ice cubes
- ½ C. unsweetened orange juice
- 1 tbsp. honey
- 1 handfuls sesame seeds
- ½ C. blueberries
- ½ C. frozen strawberries

Here's how to do it:

1. Mix everything in a blender.
2. Puree ingredients until smooth in texture or you reach your desired consistency.

5. Tart Green Monster Smoothie

Here's how to do it:

- Few ice cubes
- 1 tbsp. chia seeds
- 1 apple
- 1 handful kale
- 1 banana
- ½ - 1 C. unsweetened almond milk

Here's how to do it:

1. Mix everything in a blender.
2. Puree ingredients until smooth in texture or you reach your desired consistency.

6. Tropical Delight Smoothie

Ingredients:

- 2-3 ice cubes
- 1 C. orange juice
- 1 handful flaxseeds
- 2 kiwis
- 2 mangoes
- Half a pineapple

Here's how to do it:

1. Mix everything in a blender.
2. Puree ingredients until smooth in texture or you reach your desired consistency.

7. Cacao and Date Delight Smoothie

Ingredients:

- Pinch of cinnamon
- ½ C. unsweetened almond milk
- ¼ tsp. vanilla
- 1 tbsp. cacao powder
- 4 walnuts halves
- 5 pitted dates

Here's how to do it:

1. Mix everything in a blender.
2. Puree ingredients until smooth in texture or you reach your desired consistency.

8. Anti-Aging Mixed Berry Smoothie

Ingredients:

- 4 ice cubes
- ½ banana
- 1 tbsp. honey
- 1 tbsp. flaxseeds
- ½ C. almond milk
- ½ C. raspberries
- 1 C. blueberries

Here's how to do it:

1. Mix everything in a blender.
2. Puree ingredients until smooth in texture or you reach your desired consistency.

9. Blueberry Peach Smoothie

Ingredients:

- ¾ C. unsweetened vanilla almond milk
- 1 ½ C. sliced peaches
- ½ C. frozen blueberries

Here's how to do it:

1. Mix everything in a blender.
2. Puree ingredients until smooth in texture or you reach your desired consistency.

10. Berry Beauty Smoothie

Ingredients:

- ¼ C. water
- ¾ C. soy milk
- 1 tbsp. flaxseed
- ½ C. chopped pineapple
- ½ C. frozen mixed berries
- ¼ C. peeled/sliced kiwi
- 1 banana

Here's how to do it:

1. Mix everything in a blender.
2. Puree ingredients until smooth in texture or you reach your desired consistency.

11. Vitamin E Green Smoothie

Ingredients:

- 1 C. spinach
- ½ avocado
- ¼ C. lemon juice
- 1 C. almond milk
- ¼ C. sunflower seeds
- 1 banana

Here's how to do it:

1. Mix everything in a blender.
2. Puree ingredients until smooth in texture or you reach your desired consistency.

12. Tropically Aging Smoothie

Ingredients:

- 1 C. blueberries
- ¼ C. lemon juice
- 1 C. coconut water
- 1 C. strawberries
- Handful mint
- ¼ C. chia seeds

Here's how to do it:

1. Mix everything in a blender.
2. Puree ingredients until smooth in texture or you reach your desired consistency.

13. Leafy Anti-Aging Power Smoothie

Ingredients:

- 2 C. kale leaves
- ¼ C. lemon juice
- 2 cored apples
- 1 C. chopped carrot
- 1 C. coconut water

Here's how to do it:

1. Mix everything in a blender.
2. Puree ingredients until smooth in texture or you reach your desired consistency.

14. Chia Smoothie

Ingredients:

- 1 C. coconut water
- 2 C. mango
- 1 C. pineapple
- ¼ C. chia seeds

Here's how to do it:

1. Mix everything in a blender.
2. Puree ingredients until smooth in texture or you reach your desired consistency.

15. Cherry Shake Smoothie

Ingredients:

- ½ banana
- 2-3 C. spinach
- 1 C. cherries
- 2 tbsp. flax oil
- 1 C. coconut milk

Here's how to do it:

1. Mix everything in a blender.
2. Puree ingredients until smooth in texture or you reach your desired consistency.

Superfoods

1. Strawberry Goji Berry Smoothie

Ingredients:

- Ice
- 2 C. almond milk
- 2 tsp. honey
- 1 C. strawberries
- 2 tbsp. dried goji berries

Here's how to do it:

1. Mix everything in a blender.
2. Puree ingredients until smooth in texture or you reach your desired consistency.

2. Kick Booty Kale Smoothie

Ingredients:

- 1-3 tsp. honey
- 2 tbsp. peanut butter
- ¼ c. frozen pineapple
- ¼ C. Greek yogurt
- 1 frozen banana
- ¾ C. almond milk
- 2 C. kale

Here's how to do it:

1. Mix everything in a blender.
2. Puree ingredients until smooth in texture or you reach your desired consistency.

3. Blueberry Flax Smoothie

Ingredients:

- 1 C. coconut milk
- ¼ C. Greek yogurt
- Handful of spinach
- 1 tbsp. flaxseed
- 1 C. frozen blueberries

Here's how to do it:

1. Mix everything in a blender.
2. Puree ingredients until smooth in texture or you reach your desired consistency.

4. Spiced Green Tea Smoothie

Ingredients:

- 6-8 ice cubes
- 2 tbsp. plain yogurt
- 1 pear
- 2 tsp. honey
- Juice of 1 lemon
- 1/8 tsp. cayenne pepper
- ¾ C. chilled green tea

Here's how to do it:

1. Mix everything in a blender.
2. Puree ingredients until smooth in texture or you reach your desired consistency.

5. Antioxidant Berry Smoothie Bowl

Ingredients:

- ¼ C. pomegranate seeds
- 1 tbsp. coconut flakes
- 1 tbsp. pepitas
- 1 tsp. chia seeds
- Fresh blackberries and raspberries
- ½ banana
- ½ C. almond milk
- 1 tbsp. hemp seeds
- ½ C. frozen berries
- 1 frozen banana

Here's how to do it:

1. Mix everything in a blender.
2. Puree ingredients until smooth in texture or you reach your desired consistency.
3. Pour smoothie mixture into bowl and top with desired toppings.

6. Chocolate Avocado Smoothie

Ingredients:

- 2 C. coconut milk
- 1-2 tbsp. cocoa powder
- ½ C. frozen raspberries
- 2 frozen bananas
- 1 avocado

Here's how to do it:

1. Mix everything in a blender.
2. Puree ingredients until smooth in texture or you reach your desired consistency.

7. Plum Quinoa Smoothie

Ingredients:

- 4-5 ice cubes
- ¼ tsp. cinnamon
- 1 tsp. vanilla
- 1 C. almond milk
- ¼ C. cooked quinoa
- ½ frozen banana
- 1 pitted/chopped ripe plum

Here's how to do it:

1. Mix everything in a blender.
2. Puree ingredients until smooth in texture or you reach your desired consistency.

8. Oat Coconut Smoothie

Ingredients:

- ½ C. ice
- 1/3 C. orange juice
- 1 tbsp. honey
- 2 tbsp. coconut oil
- 1/3 C. Greek yogurt
- ¼ C. rolled oats
- ½ banana

Here's how to do it:

1. Mix everything in a blender.
2. Puree ingredients until smooth in texture or you reach your desired consistency.

9. Swamp Smoothie

Ingredients:

- 1 tbsp. hemp seeds
- 3 tbsp. hemp protein powder
- 1 tbsp. cacao powder
- 1 C. almond milk
- 1 handful spinach
- ½ C. chopped broccoli
- ½ banana
- 1 C. strawberries

Here's how to do it:

1. Mix everything in a blender.
2. Puree ingredients until smooth in texture or you reach your desired consistency.

10. Coconut Turmeric Smoothie

Ingredients:

- 1 tsp. maca
- 1 tsp. chia seeds
- ½ tsp. ginger
- ½ tsp. cinnamon
- ½ - 1 tsp. turmeric
- 1 tbsp. coconut oil
- 1 frozen banana
- ½ C. frozen pineapple
- 1 C. coconut milk

Here's how to do it:

1. Mix everything in a blender.
2. Puree ingredients until smooth in texture or you reach your desired consistency.

11. Green Apple Smoothie

Ingredients:

- 1 tbsp. chia seeds
- ½ tsp. cinnamon
- 1 tsp. minced ginger
- 1 banana
- 1 C. orange juice
- 1 apple
- 1 ½ C. kale

Here's how to do it:

1. Mix everything in a blender.
2. Puree ingredients until smooth in texture or you reach your desired consistency.

12. Babe Ruth Smoothie

Ingredients:

- 1 tbsp. chia seeds
- 1 C. spinach
- ½ C. Greek yogurt
- 2 C. orange juice
- 1 banana
- ½ C. pineapple
- 1 C. strawberries

Here's how to do it:

1. Mix everything in a blender.
2. Puree ingredients until smooth in texture or you reach your desired consistency.

13. Sweet Cherry Almond Smoothie

Ingredients:

- Ice
- 1 banana
- 1 scoop protein powder
- 1 C. almond milk
- 1 ½ C. frozen cherries

Here's how to do it:

1. Mix everything in a blender.
2. Puree ingredients until smooth in texture or you reach your desired consistency.

14. Lovely Greens Smoothie

Ingredients:

- 1 banana
- Ice
- 1 ½ C. orange juice
- ½ C. grapes
- 2 C. spinach
- 1 C. pineapple

Here's how to do it:

1. Mix everything in a blender.
2. Puree ingredients until smooth in texture or you reach your desired consistency.

15. Chocolate Powerhouse Smoothie

Ingredients:

- 1 tbsp. almond butter
- 1 banana
- 1 C. spinach
- ½ C. blueberries
- 1 scoop chocolate protein powder
- 1 C. coconut milk
- Ice

Here's how to do it:

1. Mix everything in a blender.
2. Puree ingredients until smooth in texture or you reach your desired consistency.

Conclusion

I want to congratulate you for making it to the end of *The Complete Healthy Smoothie Recipe Book.*

If you are serious about getting your health back on track and becoming the healthiest version of yourself possible, then all of these smoothie recipes will come in handy any time of day when you are crunched for time!

Stop falling victim to fat and carb-filled convenience foods and whip up a smoothie instead! As you have read, all of the smoothie recipes have something a bit different to offer your body than the next. I hope that you find a smoothie recipe for all parts of your day to help you feel better, energized, and motivated to take on life each day!

Finally, if you found this book useful in anyway, a review on Amazon is always appreciated!